How to use this book 

Follow the advice, in italics, given for you on each page.
Support the children as they read the text that is shaded in cream.
***Praise** the children at every step!*
Detailed guidance is provided in the Read Write Inc. Phonics Handbook.

9 reading activities

Children:

1. *Practise reading the speed sounds.*
2. *Read the green, red and challenge words for the non-fiction text.*
3. *Listen as you read the introduction.*
4. *Discuss the vocabulary check with you.*
5. *Read the non-fiction text.*
6. *Re-read the non-fiction text and discuss the 'questions to talk about'.*
7. *Re-read the non-fiction text with fluency and expression.*
8. *Answer the questions to 'read and answer'.*
9. *Practise reading the speed words.*

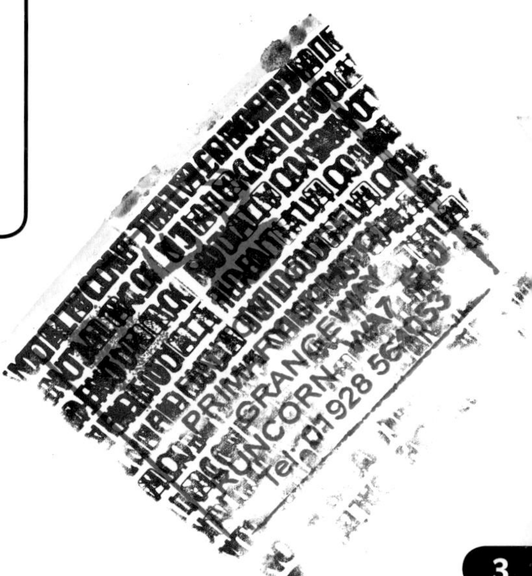

Speed sounds

Consonants *Say the pure sounds (do not add 'uh').*

f	l	m	n	r	s	v	z	sh	th	ng
ff	ll	mm	nn	rr	ss	ve	zz			nk
	le		kn	wr	**se**		s			
					c		se			
					ce					

b	c	d	g	h	j	p	qu	t	w	x	y	ch
bb	k	dd	gg			pp		tt	wh			tch
	ck											

Vowels *Say the vowel sound and then the word, eg 'a', 'at'.*

at	hen	in	on	up	day	see	high	blow
	head				make	tea	smile	home
						happy	find	no
						he		

zoo	look	car	for	fair	whirl	shout	boy
brute			door	care	nurse		spoil
blue			snore		letter		

Each box contains one sound but sometimes more than one grapheme. Focus graphemes are ***circled****.*

Green words

Read in Fred Talk (pure sounds).

beach	cream	clean	read	sea	kite	line
lie	about	swim	glass	spade	place	harm
home	close	look	fish	shirt		

Read in syllables.

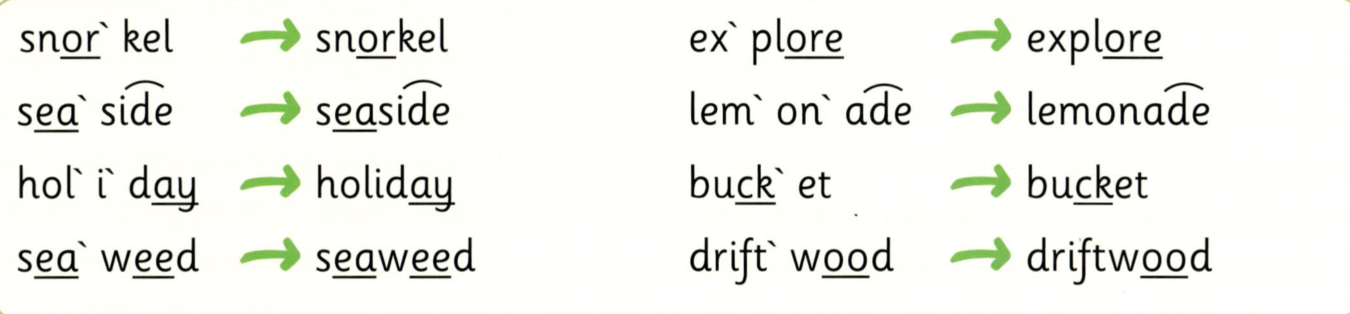

snor` kel → snorkel		ex` plore → explore	
sea` side → seaside		lem` on` ade → lemonade	
hol` i` day → holiday		buck` et → bucket	
sea` weed → seaweed		drift` wood → driftwood	

Read the root word first and then with the ending.

shake → shakes	stone → stones
seahorse → seahorses	thing → things

Red words

the you do old some your water

Challenge words

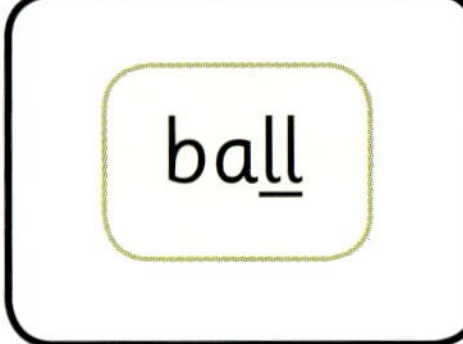

At the seaside

Written by Gill Munton

Introduction

Have you ever been to the seaside? What kinds of things can you see and do there? Do you live near the sea? This book is all about what you can do and see at the seaside.

Vocabulary check

Discuss the meaning (as used in the non-fiction text) after the children have read the word.

	definition
snorkel	*a tube you can breathe through while you swim underwater*
arm bands	*rings you wear on your arms to stop you from sinking while you learn to swim*
seaweed	*plants that grow in the sea*
driftwood	*old bits of wood carried onto the beach by the sea*
seahorses	*tiny fish with heads that look a bit like a horse's head*
T-shirt	*a summer top with short sleeves*

Punctuation to note:

!	*Exclamation marks to show that something is very important*
'	*Apostrophe to show that the word* don't *is a shortened version of* do not
-	*Hyphen between the two words in* T-shirt *to show that they are closely linked*
:	*Colon to show a list follows*
•	*Bullet point to show an item in a list*

The seaside is a good place for a holiday or a day out.

Read about the seaside in this book.

Things you can do

You can:

- dig in the sand with a bucket and a spade
- play ball games
- look in rock pools
- swim in the sea
- put on your mask and snorkel and look for fish in the sea

Always swim with an adult!

Stay close to the beach!

Put on arm bands if you can't swim yet!

- fish with a rod and line
- explore the caves
- play with a kite
- lie in the shade and read a book.

Things you can see on the beach

You can see:

crabs

shells

seahorses

seaweed

stones

starfish

old bits of pot and glass

driftwood

Collect some of those things in your bucket or net.

Hot sun can harm your skin!

Don't forget your sun cream when you play on the beach!

Put on a sunhat and a T-shirt!

Things you can eat and drink

You can eat:

- a picnic on the beach
- ice cream cones from the ice cream van
- fish and chips from the shop.

Keep our beaches clean!

Put all your rubbish in a bag and take it home with you!

You can drink:

- water
- milk shakes
- lemonade.

It's fun at the seaside!

Questions to talk about 

Re-read the page. Read the question to the children. Tell them whether it is a FIND IT *question or* PROVE IT *question.*

FIND IT	**PROVE IT**
✓ *Turn to the page*	✓ *Turn to the page*
✓ *Read the question*	✓ *Read the question*
✓ *Find the answer*	✓ *Find your evidence*
	✓ *Explain why*

Page 10:	FIND IT	*What can you put on so that you can look for fish in the sea?*
Page 11:	PROVE IT	*What should you wear in the sea if you can't swim? Why do you think this is important?*
Page 13:	PROVE IT	*Why do you think it is important to wear a sunhat and a T-shirt at the seaside?*
Page 13:	FIND IT	*What sort of cream stops the sun from harming your skin?*
Page 14:	FIND IT	*What can you buy from a van at the seaside?*
Page 15:	FIND IT	*How can you help to keep beaches clean?*

Questions to read and answer 

(Children complete without your help.)

1 What can you do at the beach?

2 What sort of wood do you see on a beach?

3 What can you find on a beach?

4 What can you put on so that the sun will not harm your skin?

5 What would you like to eat and drink at the seaside?